Contributors

Abigail Laub
Alex Verlek
Angela Van Breemen
F.C. Nolan
Caressa Walker
D. C. Gomez
Dan Jones
Daniel Lawrence Abrams
Daniel Paksi
Diane Bator
Jake Bennett
James L Hill
Joel Mckay
Karen Dustman
Pat Black Gould & Steve Hardiman
Richard Natale
Sammie Bridges
Juanita Finger
Peter Hargraves
David McGowan

Review Tales
A Book Magazine For Indie Authors

Founder & Editor in Chief: S. Jeyran Main
Publisher: Review Tales Publishing & Editing Services
Print & Distribution: Ingram Spark
Designs: Pexels
ISBN 978-1-988680-75-0 (Paperback)
ISBN 978-1-988680-74-3 (Digital)
www.jeyranmain.com
For all inquiries, please contact us directly.

Photo Credits from Pexels:
pexels-alinevianafoto-2465877
pexels-anna-kanifatova-2241048-3968446
pexels-jjskorupski-7431257
pexels-pixabay-415078

Editor's Note

Welcome to the eighth issue of Review Tales Book Review Magazine! As summer settles in with its long days and quiet, reflective evenings, we're thrilled to bring you another thoughtfully curated selection of book reviews that spotlight a diverse group of talented authors.

This issue features stories that challenge, comfort, entertain, and inspire. From debut voices to seasoned writers, each author featured in these pages offers a unique perspective, reminding us why books remain such powerful companions, especially in a season made for reading. Whether you're lounging by the lake, tucked into your favorite chair, or catching a few quiet minutes in the sun, we hope this edition offers a collection of titles that you'll want to explore and share.

We extend our heartfelt thanks to the authors and publishers who graciously participated in this issue. Your openness, creativity, and commitment to your craft are what make Review Tales possible. It is a privilege to read and highlight your work.

To our readers and supporters, thank you for being part of the Review Tales community. Each share, subscription, and word-of-mouth recommendation helps us continue to champion literature and support the broader writing community. Independent voices need places to be seen, and your continued encouragement ensures those voices are heard.

The writing world is one of dedication, solitude, and relentless hope. Behind every book is a journey of late nights, rewrites, doubt, and determination. We're honored to be a small part of that journey by offering a space for books to shine and for readers to discover stories worth holding on to.

As you dive into this summer issue, we invite you to explore new genres, champion independent authors, and find your next favorite book along the way.

Here's to stories that stay with us—this summer and beyond.

Jeyran Main

Jeyran Main
Editor-in-Chief
Book Review Magazine

Welcome

SUMMER 2025 | ISSUE 08

BOOK
REVIEWS

Review Tales is thrilled to have reached the milestone of over 2000 book reviews. With this extensive experience, we've had the privilege of exploring a vast range of literature. Our reviews are always impartial and thoughtfully crafted to highlight authors' strengths while inspiring them to keep creating. For this summer issue, we've handpicked exceptional book reviews to feature.

TO APPLY FOR A BOOK REVIEW VISIT
WWW.JEYRANMAIN.COM

Book Reviews

ABBY AND THE BICYCLE RACE: A GIRL, A RACE, AND AN UNSTOPPABLE SPIRIT BY ABIGAIL SUBRENA LAUB

COACHING MASTERY IN SIXTY QUESTIONS BY ALEX VERLEK

REVENGE IS NOT ENOUGH BY ANGELA VAN BREEMEN

CAGED BY F. C. NOLAN

THE SCROLLS OF THE MOUNTAIN GUARDIAN BY CARESSA WALKER

A DESPERATE CAT LADY BY D. C. GOMEZ

THE GREEN MAN BY DAN JONES

IMMORTALITY BYTES BY DANIEL LAWRENCE ABRAMS

THE CHOSEN ONE BY DANIEL PAKSI

DIAMOND ON THE ROCKS BY DIANE BATOR

LUNARMANCER BY JAKE BENNETT

THE RUBY CRADLE BY JAMES L. HILL

THE DUNGEONEERS AND THE TREASURE OF ROAN BY JOEL MCKAY

MIAMI'S GREAT HURRICANE BY KAREN DUSTMAN

ALL THE BROKEN ANGELS BY PAT BLACK-GOULD & STEVE HARDIMAN

GREENWICH CONNECTION BY RICHARD NATALE

FEAR OF REPERCUSSION BY SAMMIE BRIDGES

EXECUTIVE FUNCTIONING FOR TEENS MADE SIMPLE BY JUANITA FINGER

SAFE HAVEN BY PETER HARGRAVES

PARTNER BY DAVID M. MCGOWAN

ABBY AND THE BICYCLE RACE: A GIRL, A RACE, AND AN UNSTOPPABLE SPIRIT

Abigail Subrena Laub

Reviewer: Jeyran Main

Abby and the Bicycle Race is a charming and empowering picture book that delivers a powerful message with warmth, authenticity, and heart. Based on author Abigail Subrena Laub's childhood experiences in Guyana, this uplifting tale highlights courage, self-belief, and the importance of challenging societal expectations, especially for young girls.

Set against the colorful backdrop of a bustling Sunday morning at the Annual Festival, the story draws readers into a vivid world filled with excitement, delicious food, and the joy of community. Young Abby, dressed in her favorite pink dress and white shoes, is ready for a day of celebration with her cousin Fazie. But when she discovers that the town's bicycle race is only for boys, her excitement is quickly replaced with disappointment.

What follows is an inspiring journey of bold determination. Rather than accepting the limitation placed on her, Abby decides to join the race anyway, scuffed knees and all. Her courage to stand up and challenge tradition not only shifts the tone of the story but invites readers to reflect on their capabilities and the value of perseverance.

Laub's writing is engaging, accessible, and emotionally resonant. She doesn't shy away from depicting the societal constraints that children—especially girls—often face, but does so in a way that feels age-appropriate and hopeful. The narrative arc is satisfying and triumphant, making Abby an unforgettable character whose spirit will stay with readers long after the final page.

Y. Sanders' illustrations add an extra layer of richness to the book. Bright, expressive, and full of movement, the visuals beautifully complement the story, bringing the streets of Guyana to life. Abby's expressions, the vibrant festival scenes, and the exhilarating energy of the race are all captured with detail and heart.

At its core, Abby and the Bicycle Race is a story about self-worth, bravery, and disrupting gender norms. It encourages children to question the world around them and to believe in their ability to create change. This book would make a valuable addition to any classroom, library, or home bookshelf.

Whether read aloud to a group or cherished one-on-one, Abby's story is a celebration of grit and girlhood—and a reminder that every child has the power to race toward their dreams.

COACHING MASTERY IN SIXTY QUESTIONS

Alex Verlek

Reviewer: Jeyran Main

Coaching Mastery in Sixty Questions by Alex Verlek is a reflective, insightful, and deeply authentic exploration of the coaching profession, written with generosity, humility, and a touch of personal celebration. Marking the author's 60th birthday, the book becomes more than just a professional manual—it's a heartfelt offering from a seasoned Master Certified Coach who genuinely seeks to "pay it forward."

Structured around 60 real questions posed by coaches and coaching enthusiasts, the book reads like a rich dialogue. Each question opens the door to a thoughtful, experience-based response that blends practical advice with philosophical depth. Verlek doesn't simply teach; he invites readers into a co-creative reflection on what coaching is, what it can become, and how to navigate its complexities with grace.

What sets this book apart is its tone—warm, honest, and refreshingly human. Verlek shares his own experiences, doubts, and missteps without hesitation. Whether discussing being ghosted by a coachee or exploring the implications of AI in coaching, he brings vulnerability and curiosity to the page. His transparency allows readers to feel less alone in their journeys, while his wisdom shines through in gentle but firm reminders about boundaries, ethics, and professional development.

The metaphor of the garden, used early in the book to describe the coaching process, is particularly memorable. It beautifully encapsulates the dynamic between coach and coachee: a shared walk, a shared vision, the uncovering of tools, and the willingness to dig in. Verlek's language throughout is vivid and often poetic, making the book not only instructive but also inspiring.

This book also stands out for its balanced view on current topics, such as the role of AI in coaching, internal coaching in organizations, and how to market coaching services with integrity. His perspective remains grounded in values like trust, authenticity, and mutual respect—qualities that are increasingly vital in a world of quick fixes and shortcuts.

Whether you're a new coach seeking direction, an experienced practitioner looking to reconnect with your purpose, or simply curious about the power of coaching, Coaching Mastery in Sixty Questions offers rich nourishment. It's a rare blend of head, heart, and hands—a manual, a memoir, and a manifesto all in one.

Ultimately, Alex Verlek reminds us that coaching is not about having all the answers, but about learning to ask better questions—and to listen, always, with presence.

REVENGE IS NOT ENOUGH
Angela Van Breemen

Reviewer: Jeyran Main

Revenge is Not Enough is a taut and emotionally charged historical thriller that explores the devastating aftermath of war, the burdens of guilt, and the long shadow of revenge. Set in the smoldering ruins of post–World War I Britain, this gripping novel follows the fractured lives of soldiers, spies, and survivors as they struggle to piece together a future haunted by the past.

At the center of the story is the compelling protagonist, Walter—an emotionally scarred former soldier turned intelligence officer, whose tormented sense of justice fuels his pursuit of truth. When a friend is brutally murdered under suspicious circumstances, Walter is pulled into a complex investigation that unravels not only secrets from the war but also the tangled motivations of those closest to him. What begins as a mission of justice soon spirals into a journey of moral ambiguity, personal reckoning, and emotional vulnerability.

The novel excels in blending meticulous historical detail with taut psychological drama. Through atmospheric prose, the author transports readers into a postwar London that feels raw, brittle, and morally compromised. The writing balances the grit of espionage and violence with the quiet devastation of grief, love, and unspoken trauma. Whether in the smoky corners of intelligence offices or the desolate streets of bombed-out cities, the setting hums with tension and unease.

What elevates Revenge is Not Enough beyond the typical historical thriller is its emotional depth. Characters are not just pawns in a spy narrative—they are fully realized, conflicted people whose personal traumas shape every decision. Walter, in particular, stands out. His introspective voice, laced with regret and yearning, gives the novel a poignant anchor. His relationships with colleagues, lovers, and adversaries are complex and genuine, marked by silences and unresolved wounds that ring true.

Themes of betrayal, justice, and redemption echo through every chapter. The novel challenges the very premise of revenge as a form of closure, suggesting instead that healing must come from honesty and emotional reckoning, rather than retaliation.

Fans of Robert Harris, C.J. Sansom, or Sebastian Faulks will find much to admire here. With its compelling mix of espionage, historical intrigue, and psychological complexity, Revenge is Not Enough is both an immersive page-turner and a thoughtful exploration of what it means to survive—and confront—the traumas of war.

CAGED
F. C. Nolan

Reviewer: Jeyran Main

TIME TO START A NEW TRILOGY
Maven

Caged by F.C. Nolan is a powerful and unflinching contemporary novel that explores the lifelong consequences of trauma, the complexities of justice, and the raw, quiet strength required to survive. Told in intimate prose and anchored by a compelling, deeply human narrator, this novel doesn't just tell a story—it compels readers to feel it in their bones.

At the heart of the novel is Libby, a woman whose life has been irrevocably shaped by a single, violent moment in her past. Now, decades later, her abuser is up for parole, and Libby must decide whether to face him, confront her past, and reclaim her voice in a justice system that often fails survivors. What unfolds is not a revenge tale, but a reckoning—an exploration of grief, guilt, healing, and the meaning of freedom, both literal and emotional.

Nolan's writing is hauntingly beautiful—sparse yet evocative, capturing the nuances of trauma with grace and empathy. She portrays Libby not as a victim, but as a layered, evolving woman navigating the rugged terrain of memory, forgiveness, and agency. As Libby prepares a victim impact statement, the novel slowly unveils the full weight of what happened to her—and how it has shaped every relationship, every silence, every choice since.

One of the book's most striking achievements is its ability to convey the emotional complexity of survival. There are no easy answers here—just a deeply personal journey through shame, anger, strength, and sorrow. Nolan also weaves in a subtle commentary on systemic failures—how legal processes often retraumatize survivors, and how society's definitions of closure and justice rarely reflect the lived experience of those most affected.

Supporting characters—Libby's husband, her adult daughter, and the wider community—are drawn with care, revealing how trauma reverberates beyond the individual. Yet this remains Libby's story, and her voice is one of the novel's greatest strengths: vulnerable, honest, and quietly fierce.

Caged is both a meditation and a mirror. It does not offer a traditional resolution, but it offers something more meaningful: truth. For readers who appreciated Room, The Lovely Bones, or A Man Called Ove, this novel will resonate deeply.

F.C. Nolan has written a story that is not only timely but necessary—a testament to survival, voice, and the unbreakable human spirit.

THE SCROLLS OF THE MOUNTAIN GUARDIAN

Caressa Walker

Reviewer: Jeyran Main

The Scrolls of the Mountain Guardian is an imaginative and thrilling middle-grade fantasy adventure that marks an exciting debut for author Caressa Walker. With the promise of a series in the making, this first installment introduces readers to Mei Haroshi, a brave and determined young girl who becomes the unlikely hero of her village.

Set against the enchanting backdrop of Mount Tsuru, the story begins with Mei stumbling upon ancient scrolls that speak of a mythical dragon hidden deep within the mountain. These scrolls not only spark her curiosity but also set the wheels in motion for an epic journey. When a mysterious cosmic event begins to threaten the peace of her homeland, Mei realizes that her discovery might hold the key to saving everything she loves.

What makes Mei such a compelling protagonist is her ability to balance vulnerability and strength. She is relatable to young readers, yet her courage and determination inspire admiration. As Mei sets out to awaken the legendary dragon, she must overcome treacherous terrain, confront ancient trials, and uncover secrets long buried by time. Each challenge she faces serves as a metaphor for growth, resilience, and the discovery of one's inner strength.

Caressa Walker's storytelling is vibrant and full of heart. Her descriptive writing brings Mei's world to life with rich detail, from the mystical landscape of Mount Tsuru to the quiet strength of the village she hopes to protect. The pacing is well-balanced, blending suspense and introspection in a way that will keep middle-grade readers engaged from start to finish.

One of the book's greatest strengths is its message. At its core, The Scrolls of the Mountain Guardian is a story about courage, destiny, and self-belief, even when the path ahead is uncertain. It celebrates the power of curiosity and the importance of protecting ancient wisdom, all while delivering the kind of adventurous fun that young readers crave.

As the first book in a planned series, this novel leaves readers eager to find out what's next for Mei Haroshi and the secrets still hidden within Mount Tsuru. It's a strong start to what promises to be a magical, meaningful, and memorable journey.

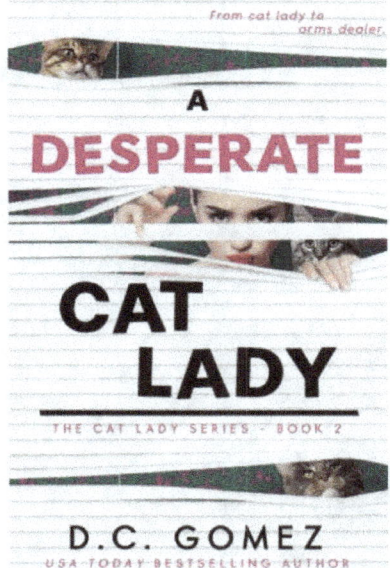

A DESPERATE CAT LADY

D. C. Gomez

Reviewer: Jeyran Main

A Desperate Cat Lady is an honest, spirited, and often darkly humorous memoir about one woman's battle with mental illness, addiction, homelessness, and her complicated but vital relationship with a group of stray cats who, in many ways, saved her life. What begins as a tale of loss and desperation unfolds into a story of unlikely resilience and emotional survival, told with unflinching candor and unexpected wit.

D. C. Gomez details her spiral into poverty after a series of personal, professional, and medical setbacks. Unemployed, evicted, and adrift in a world that offers little mercy to the vulnerable, she finds herself taking shelter in her car with only a few possessions and the company of her feline companions. The narrative doesn't shy away from the harsh realities of her existence: hunger, anxiety, humiliation, and the brutal indifference of bureaucracy and social services.

Yet what sets this memoir apart is its refusal to collapse under the weight of its sorrow. The tone is raw but never self-pitying. There are moments of piercing insight, hilarious asides, and even pockets of joy amid the chaos. The cats themselves become characters—demanding, loyal, mischievous, and utterly necessary. They are not just pets or metaphors, but fellow survivors, each with their personality and importance in Gomez's life.

In this sense, A Desperate Cat Lady becomes more than a personal memoir—it is a reflection on the fragile boundaries between despair and connection, between invisibility and being seen. It also offers a biting critique of the societal systems that fail people when they need help most.

Gomez's prose is conversational, confessional, and occasionally poetic, drawing readers into her world without artifice. While the structure leans toward stream-of-consciousness at times, it mirrors the mental state of someone navigating trauma, medication, and survival with limited support.

This is a book for readers who appreciate memoirs like The Glass Castle or Educated—gritty, intimate accounts of life on the margins, told with heart and humor. It may especially resonate with those who understand the healing power of animals and the quiet strength it takes to endure when everything is stacked against you.

A Desperate Cat Lady is a fierce, funny, and moving story of resilience, told through the eyes of someone who knows what it means to be truly desperate—and to still show up for the creatures who depend on her.

THE GREEN MAN
Dan Jones

Reviewer: Jeyran Main

The Green Man is a richly imagined and thought-provoking medieval mystery that blends historical fiction with eerie, otherworldly tension. Written by Dan Jones, a musician, podcaster, and Head of European Space Agency Policy, this novel showcases a mind deeply attuned to both grand imagination and intellectual precision. Readers drawn to The Name of the Rose, The Essex Serpent, or even The X-Files will find a compelling spiritual kinship here.

The story follows Brother Jacobus of Venna, a Dominican inquisitor with a sharp intellect and a rebellious streak. After publicly humiliating another inquisitor during a witch trial in Italy, Jacobus is drawn to troubling rumors coming out of northern England. Against the wishes of the Church hierarchy in Avignon, he ventures to Berwick, a turbulent region straddling the medieval fault lines of English and Scottish conflict.

What he finds is a society in turmoil: children vanishing under mysterious circumstances, fear clinging to the woods, and locals bound by silence. Friars remain tight-lipped, raiders scour the countryside, and a creeping dread seems to hover just out of reach. As Jacobus digs deeper, he is forced to confront questions of reason, faith, and the blurred boundaries between the natural and supernatural.

Jones's prose is tight, atmospheric, and expertly researched. He paints the medieval world not with the glossy romanticism of fantasy but with its gritty reality—political unrest, religious fractures, and the human yearning for meaning amid chaos. Yet, beneath the realism lies a disturbing and poetic mystery that lingers like mist over ancient ruins.

What truly elevates The Green Man is its relevance. While the setting is the 14th century, its exploration of truth, power, and institutional blind spots resonates powerfully with today's political and cultural climate. Readers will find themselves reflecting on modern parallels even as they are transported back centuries.

Dan Jones is no stranger to storytelling, with a successful sci-fi debut (Man O'War), a prominent podcast (Chronscast), and a musical career with the prog-metal band Sky Empire. His diverse creative background enriches this novel with rhythm, vision, and philosophical depth.

IMMORTALITY BYTES
Daniel Lawrence Abrams

Reviewer: Jeyran Main

Immortality Bytes: Digital Minds Don't Get Hungry is a razor-sharp, cyberpunk adventure that blends dark humor, philosophical depth, and satirical bite into a fast-paced narrative bursting with originality. Daniel Lawrence Abrams's debut novel is as entertaining as it is thought-provoking, delivering a high-concept story that's both wildly imaginative and eerily plausible.

Set in a near-future society dominated by AI, universal basic income, and pod-based lifestyles, the novel introduces us to Stu Reigns—an idealistic, semi-slacker hacker who dreams of more than digital distractions and passive existence. Stu's quiet ambitions take a turn when his brilliant ex, Roxy Zhang, invents a technology that makes digital immortality possible. As news of her breakthrough spreads, power-hungry elites, corrupt tycoons, and underground operatives begin circling.

Chief among them is Chuck Rosti, a terminally ill billionaire and financial criminal who wants to cheat death—and justice—by uploading himself before he's imprisoned. With the help of coercion, manipulation, and a global web of deceit, Rosti sets his sights on Stu and Roxy's discovery. What follows is an "inverted heist" full of unpredictable turns, tech-fueled chaos, and moments of surprising heart.

Abrams' writing shines with crisp dialogue and pitch-perfect pacing. The story's humor is biting, often reminiscent of Douglas Adams but layered with a darker, more cyberpunk edge. The world-building is immersive and disturbingly believable, touching on issues like tech monopolies, surveillance, and what it means to be human in a digitized society.

What elevates Immortality Bytes beyond genre conventions is its emotional and intellectual core. Amidst digital clones, mob entanglements, and near-future absurdities, Stu's journey is ultimately one of self-discovery, purpose, and morality in a world where even consciousness can be commodified. Supporting characters—ranging from a shrewd Southern matriarch to Russian gangsters—add texture and unexpected poignancy.

The accolades speak for themselves: multiple awards including "Best Sci-Fi: Cyberpunk" (American Fiction Awards), "Best Humor/Satire" (Storytrade Awards), and glowing reviews from Kirkus, Publishers Weekly's BookLife, and Reader Views all point to a breakout success.

THE CHOSEN ONE
Daniel Paksi

Reviewer: Jeyran Main

The Chosen One, the first English translation of Daniel Paksi's debut novel, is a spellbinding blend of classic fantasy storytelling and philosophical reflection. Initially published in 1998 and now available to English-speaking readers for the first time, the novel marks the beginning of a distinguished academic and intellectual journey. Paksi, a philosopher by profession, crafts a tale that goes beyond swords and prophecy—it questions fate, power, and the human will to resist oppression.

At the heart of this young adult fantasy is a legend rooted in divine tension. Thirteen Banner Lords rule the material world, having risen to power by divine sanction. But every so often—during what is known as the Year of the Repartition—God bestows freedom upon the world by allowing the birth of a singular child. This child is different. Blessed with a fragment of the One God's infinite power, they alone can challenge the tyrannical grip of the Banner Lords. Yet, their identity remains unknown—gender, appearance, and birthplace hidden even from the divine vicars they are meant to defy.

Paksi's premise is both familiar and fresh. While it echoes the traditional "chosen one" trope found in epic fantasy, it is given depth through the lens of philosophical inquiry. The story doesn't just unfold with action and high-stakes adventure; it asks enduring questions: Can destiny coexist with free will? Are rulers truly sanctioned by the divine, or is their authority a human construct? Is true freedom even possible under such a rule?

The narrative is lyrical and immersive, with a rich mythos and a sense of timelessness that evokes Tolkien and Le Guin, yet remains uniquely Paksi's own. The writing is poetic without being opaque, offering just enough intrigue to keep readers turning pages while inviting them to linger on more profound meanings.

What makes The Chosen One especially compelling is its resonance across generations. Readers of all ages will find value here, whether they seek a thrilling fantasy or a philosophical allegory. The novel also stands as a poignant reminder of literature's power to serve as both mirror and lamp: reflecting our world while illuminating possibilities beyond it.

DIAMOND ON THE ROCKS
Diane Bator

Reviewer: Jeyran Main

Diamond on the Rocks is a witty and engaging mystery brimming with charm, snark, and a healthy dose of small-town intrigue. Diane Bator crafts a delightful whodunit that keeps readers guessing while offering a clever, satirical lens on ambition, gossip, reinvention, and the often-comical contrast between big-city glam and small-town life.

The story centers around Lucie Rizzo, a fashionista with a sharp tongue and an unexpectedly keen eye for detail, who's attempting to restart her life in the sleepy town of Banford. She's fled a toxic relationship and a media scandal in New York City, hoping to quietly reestablish herself by working for a luxury fashion label. But her plans for anonymity are quickly dashed when a murder disrupts the local peace, and Lucie finds herself entangled in a web of suspicion, secrets, and sparkling stones that even her designer heels can't outrun.

Bator's narrative voice is fresh and punchy, with Lucie's inner monologue offering laugh-out-loud moments and biting observations on everything from provincial politics to high-end handbags. The setting of Banford is vividly drawn—a quirky, gossipy town filled with colorful characters who both help and hinder Lucie's amateur sleuthing efforts. From nosy neighbors to cryptic shopkeepers, everyone has a story—and a motive.

What sets Diamond on the Rocks apart from standard cozy mysteries is its modern tone and sharply drawn protagonist. Lucie isn't your typical small-town heroine; she's complicated, fashion-savvy, emotionally guarded, and unafraid to speak her mind. But beneath the sarcasm and stilettos is a woman struggling with trust, identity, and the pressure to prove she's more than a headline or a high-fashion disaster. Her growth throughout the novel feels authentic, making her both entertaining and relatable.

The mystery itself is well-paced and satisfyingly layered. Bator peppers the narrative with red herrings, witty banter, and just enough danger to keep the tension high without veering into grim or gritty territory. The dialogue sparkles, and the plot twists keep the pages turning. Fans of Janet Evanovich, Meg Cabot, or Elle Cosimano will feel right at home in Bator's blend of humor, heart, and sleuthing.

Ultimately, Diamond on the Rocks is not just about solving a murder—it's about reclaiming identity, building community, and navigating the rocks life throws your way with grit and glitter. Diane Bator delivers an irresistible gem of a read that sparkles with wit, mystery, and character.

LUNARMANCER
Jake Bennett

Reviewer: Jeyran Main

Lunarmancer is an ambitious and richly layered fantasy that blends magical transformation, epic adventure, and profound personal discovery. At the center is Reika, a human servant whose life is shattered after a brutal attack awakens a mysterious, moon-bound curse within her, transforming her into a weredragon and thrusting her into a world she never chose to inhabit.

Exiled from Carthage, a city ruled by anthropomorphic Metazoans, Reika embarks on a high-stakes journey across the continent of Perusia. Her goal is to find the legendary Anodyne Stone—a mythical artifact said to dispel curses. What begins as a desperate flight for freedom quickly becomes an epic quest filled with ancient powers, fractured alliances, and enemies who seek to harness or destroy the creature within her.

The world of Lunarmancer is vibrant and immersive. Author Jake Bennett introduces a cast of dynamic, multifaceted characters who each bring tension and heart to Reika's journey. From Melito, a dethroned prince seeking redemption, to Junayd, the heroic wielder of the Draco Ferrum, and Zane, who manipulates time itself, each adds depth to the adventure. Layered relationships, betrayals, and emotional struggles turn this from a standard fantasy quest into something far more resonant.

Reika's transformation is the soul of the story. Her rise from oppressed servant to empowered sorceress is both thrilling and heartbreaking. As a Lunarmancer—a rare sorceress whose strength is drawn from moonlight—she must learn to master her curse before it consumes her. The story doesn't shy away from the emotional cost of power or the inner battles Reika faces as she wrestles with identity, rage, and self-worth.

The climax builds toward an intense showdown with Destrian, a ruthless general serving the Dark Lady Tahpenes. Through prophecy, loss, and hard-won alliance, Reika must decide not only the fate of her curse but the fate of Perusia itself. It's a powerful conclusion, filled with action and meaning, while leaving space for future tales.

Lushly written and emotionally charged, Lunarmancer is a standout in the fantasy genre—one that explores what it means to carry power, confront pain, and choose your destiny.

THE RUBY CRADLE
James L. Hill

Reviewer: Jeyran Main

The Ruby Cradle is a captivating blend of historical mystery, gothic drama, and generational intrigue that unravels its secrets with poetic precision. Set in a richly imagined 19th-century English manor house, this atmospheric novel immerses readers in a world of buried truths, eerie heirlooms, and women struggling against the rigid expectations of their time.

The story follows Jane, a young and perceptive nurse who arrives at Belvedere House in 1878 to care for a traumatized mother and her newborn baby. From her first steps inside the manor, Jane senses that something is deeply wrong. The house creaks with secrets, weighed down by a legacy of grief, silence, and untold stories. At the heart of it all is a mysterious ruby cradle—an ornate heirloom that seems to carry not just a history, but a presence. Sitting ominously in the nursery, the cradle becomes both symbol and catalyst for the darkness that lingers in the house.

Told through dual timelines, the novel shifts between Jane's present and the journal of Nell, a woman from a generation earlier whose voice reaches across time to challenge, warn, and connect. This interplay is handled with remarkable grace, allowing revelations from one timeline to cast new meaning over the other. As Jane delves deeper into the family's past, she uncovers generational wounds, hidden betrayals, and a web of emotional repression that threatens to consume those still living.

The prose is lyrical and deeply evocative, filled with rich, sensory detail that brings the setting to life —from the damp chill of stone walls to the flicker of candlelight in long-forgotten corridors. The pacing is steady and deliberate, drawing the reader into its intricate emotional tapestry as it slowly unravels the mystery at its core.

What sets The Ruby Cradle apart is its exploration of motherhood, identity, loss, and the silencing of women's voices across generations. It asks difficult questions about duty, inheritance, and how trauma can be unknowingly passed down. The Ruby Cradle becomes a haunting emblem of privilege, pressure, and emotional burden disguised as legacy.

Fans of Kate Morton, Sarah Waters, or Daphne du Maurier will find much to admire here. This is historical fiction at its most atmospheric and emotionally intelligent—a slow-burning, beautifully written novel that lingers long after the final page. The Ruby Cradle is not just a mystery—it's a story of memory, resilience, and the healing power of truth.

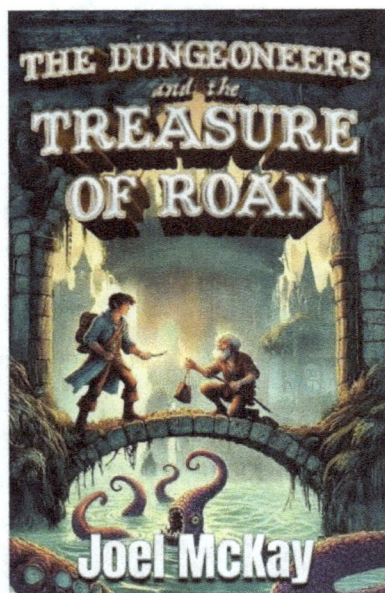

THE DUNGEONEERS AND THE TREASURE OF ROAN

Joel McKay

Reviewer: Jeyran Main

The Dungeoneers and the Treasure of Roan by Joel McKay flips the traditional dungeon crawler on its head with a thrilling, satirical, and surprisingly heartfelt novella that blends classic fantasy tropes with corporate cynicism and biting wit. It's a rare fantasy read that feels both familiar and refreshingly original—part love letter, part takedown of the genre itself.

The story unfolds in a vividly imagined yet brutal high-fantasy world where dungeons aren't mythical anomalies—they're products of a regulated, corporate-run industry. Heroes no longer seek glory; they're contracted, ranked, and discarded like disposable office interns. At the center is an unpolished but endearing squad of C-list adventurers, sent into a dungeon under vague managerial oversight—ill-prepared, disillusioned, and marching toward near-certain disaster. What follows is a mission both hilarious and blood-soaked, spiraling into chaos in all the best ways.

McKay's strength lies in his tight, economical storytelling. The novella format suits him perfectly, offering fast-paced action and razor-sharp dialogue without overstaying its welcome. Beneath the humor and carnage lies a biting critique of bureaucracy, capitalism, and toxic workplace culture—all filtered through a lens of swords and sorcery. Think The Office meets Dungeons & Dragons, with a splash of Glengarry Glen Ross.

The characters are drawn with both satire and sincerity. From burned-out veterans to overeager rookies, each reflects real-world frustrations—trapped in systems they barely understand, pushed toward failure in the name of productivity. Yet amid the cynicism, flickers of humanity shine through: loyalty, fear, courage, and unexpected camaraderie.

McKay's humor is dry, dark, and often laugh-out-loud funny—but never undercuts the story's emotional weight. The ending, brutal and unflinching, lands with thematic force—an indictment of the systems that chew people up in the name of profit and spectacle.

The Dungeoneers and the Treasure of Roan is a must-read for fantasy fans craving something sharp, subversive, and bright. It will particularly resonate with anyone who's ever navigated a broken system—whether in a cubicle or a campaign gone off the rails. This isn't just a dungeon crawl—it's a darkly comic examination of what happens when fantasy becomes commodified and the quest loses its meaning.

With grit, humor, and a timely gut-punch, Joel McKay's debut earns its place beside the likes of Terry Pratchett, Joe Abercrombie, and The Boys. Short, sharp, and viciously clever.

MIAMI'S GREAT HURRICANE

Karen Dustman

Reviewer: Jeyran Main

Karen Dustman's Miami's Great Hurricane is a gripping and masterfully written historical narrative that brings one of America's deadliest natural disasters vividly to life. With journalistic precision, emotional depth, and a novelist's eye for detail, Dustman chronicles the catastrophic storm that struck Miami in 1926 and reshaped both the city and the lives of those who endured it.

From the opening pages, Dustman plunges readers into the roaring chaos of the Category 4 hurricane that hit South Florida with devastating force. But this book isn't just about weather patterns or destruction—it's about people. Through firsthand survivor accounts, archived newspapers, and family stories, she reconstructs the lived experience of a city blindsided by nature and wholly unprepared for its wrath.

What elevates Miami's Great Hurricane beyond traditional disaster history is the careful attention to human resilience. We meet families who weathered the storm, huddled in homes that were torn apart; rescue workers, overwhelmed by the sheer scale of the damage; and everyday Floridians who pulled together in the face of unimaginable loss. The result is not just a chronicle of destruction, but a tribute to courage, ingenuity, and community.

Dustman's writing is clear, evocative, and emotionally resonant. Her background as a journalist and historian shines through in her ability to blend hard facts with storytelling flair. She also includes photos, maps, and period headlines that enhance the historical texture, offering both a visual and intellectual immersion in 1920s Miami.

The book also explores the broader implications of the storm—how it halted Florida's land boom, reshaped migration patterns, and laid bare the vulnerabilities of rapid urban expansion. In this way, Miami's Great Hurricane is not only a compelling slice of history but also a cautionary tale, reminding modern readers of the ongoing threat posed by climate and infrastructure imbalance.

This work will appeal to fans of Erik Larson, David McCullough, and anyone fascinated by American history, natural disasters, or urban development. It's particularly timely given today's climate crisis, serving as both a memorial and a warning.

In sum, Miami's Great Hurricane is deeply researched, emotionally engaging, and historically significant. Karen Dustman has given us a powerful, essential record of a moment that defined Miami—and a testament to the strength of the people who survived it.

ALL THE BROKEN ANGELS
Pat Black-Gould & Steve Hardiman

Reviewer: Jeyran Main

All the Broken Angels is a compelling and emotionally resonant work of historical fiction that traces the intertwined lives of two cousins, Cate and Albie, as they come of age in the turbulent 1960s and '70s.

Raised under the watchful eyes of their traditional Catholic family and stern school nuns in New Jersey, Cate and Albie share an unshakable bond. But when the Vietnam War erupts, their paths diverge dramatically. Albie, driven by faith and a deep sense of patriotism, enlists and is deployed to a coastal base in Southeast Asia—nicknamed Paradise. Meanwhile, Cate rejects the ideals of her upbringing, immersing herself in the bohemian counterculture of New York's Greenwich Village and living in the gritty heart of Hell's Kitchen.

As tragedy strikes and Cate's world begins to unravel, she finds strength in an unlikely group of allies—artists, activists, and veterans—who help her begin a journey of healing and personal transformation. Her resilience is tested as she navigates the emotional wreckage of war, the evolving movements of feminism and LGBTQ+ rights, and the tension between rebellion, faith, and identity.

Pat Black-Gould and Steve Hardiman craft a story that captures both the spirit and scars of a generation. Through richly drawn characters and vivid settings, they examine the emotional toll of war, the power of kinship and chosen family, and the enduring struggle to reconcile personal beliefs with a changing world.

Winner of multiple literary awards, including the 2025 Feathered Quill Literary Award and the 2024 Indies Today Award for Historical Fiction, All the Broken Angels is more than a nostalgic look back—it's a powerful exploration of love, loss, and the courage to define one's own path.

Perfect for readers who enjoy historical fiction with strong female leads, stories of social transformation, and unforgettable characters that linger long after the final page.

GREENWICH CONNECTION
Richard Natale

Reviewer: Jeyran Main

Richard Natale's Greenwich Connection is a heartfelt tribute to one of America's most iconic cultural enclaves—New York's Greenwich Village. Blending novella and interconnected short stories, this literary mosaic chronicles the dreams, heartbreaks, and quiet triumphs of eccentrics, artists, and outsiders across six transformative decades of American history.

The book opens with the novella "In the Fall of Forty-Four," beginning in war-torn Naples during the American occupation, before shifting to post-WWII New York—a city alive with reinvention, creative ambition, and emotional reckoning. At its center is a turbulent yet passionate relationship that evolves with the sweeping cultural and political changes of the late 20th century.

The stories that follow cast a light on peripheral characters first introduced in the novella, each one revealing a different angle of Village life. These aren't mere side tales—they are vivid, standalone portraits of immigrants, LGBTQ+ pioneers, artists, laborers, and dreamers. Their lives intertwine and overlap, reflecting the neighborhood's enduring role as a haven for the unconventional and the courageous.

What sets Greenwich Connection apart is Natale's ability to capture the spirit of a place that has always stood at the cultural margins, yet influenced the heart of America. His characters are richly drawn—flawed, hopeful, disillusioned, defiant—and each one resonates with emotional truth. Through their lives, the book mirrors the era-defining movements they live through: civil rights, the sexual revolution, the rise of counterculture, the devastation of AIDS, and the aftermath of 9/11.

Natale's prose is elegant yet conversational, layered with nostalgia, wit, and tenderness. His storytelling has a lived-in quality, as though you're walking beside his characters through cobblestone streets, smoky cafés, and rent-controlled apartments brimming with history.

Most powerful is the book's quietly resonant message: that even in a world marked by division and displacement, places like Greenwich Village endure as symbols of chosen family, freedom, and belonging. Through love, loss, identity, and survival, Natale reminds us that community is not built solely on blood or geography, but on the courage to be seen and the grace to see others.

Greenwich Connection is both a love letter to a neighborhood and a stirring reflection on what it means to find home in unlikely places.

FEAR OF REPERCUSSION
Sammie Bridges

Reviewer: Jeyran Main

Sammie Bridges' Fear of Repercussion is a harrowing yet tender exploration of trauma, recovery, and the quiet resilience it takes to heal. Told with unfiltered emotional honesty, the novel follows Jenny, a young woman trying to piece together a life fractured by unspoken pain and buried secrets. The story opens in a moment of deep personal collapse—Jenny alone, overwhelmed by guilt and fear, lost in the shadows of her past. What unfolds is a gripping portrait of how trauma can shape identity, distort self-worth, and stall even the most hopeful new beginnings. Through Jenny's intensely personal lens, Bridges immerses readers in the experience of someone fighting to reclaim both her voice and her future.

Jenny's childhood at The Orchard Children's Home is portrayed with a mix of warmth and horror. Though the home offered structure and a sense of belonging, it also became the setting for a trauma so profound that Jenny could not name it—let alone speak of it—without risking emotional and physical safety. As she ages out of the system and steps into adulthood, her past continues to haunt her. A new job, new friendships, and a blossoming relationship with Billy—a steady, kind-hearted man—offer glimmers of hope. Yet even as life begins to open up, Jenny remains trapped by the silence she's carried for so long.

Bridges masterfully captures the emotional contradictions of healing: the push and pull between wanting connection and fearing it, between joy and shame, between survival and the longing to truly live. Jenny's inner voice is rendered with heartbreaking clarity—fragile but persistent, raw yet compelling. It's this voice that gives the novel its emotional power.

As Jenny's carefully constructed new life begins to crack under the weight of her unspoken past, the fallout is devastating. But in that unraveling lies a turning point. With Billy's unwavering support, Jenny begins the slow, painful work of confronting her trauma, exposing long-held truths, and fighting back—not just against external threats but against her fear and self-doubt.

Fear of Repercussion is more than a story of survival—it's a moving testament to the strength it takes to choose healing, to speak the truth, and to believe, even after everything, that life can still be lived.

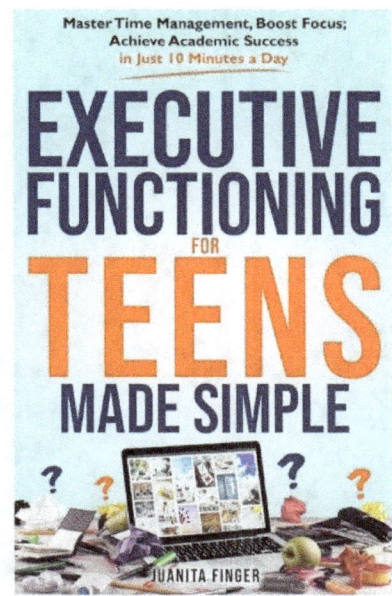

EXECUTIVE FUNCTIONING FOR TEENS MADE SIMPLE

Juanita Finger

Reviewer: Jeyran Main

In a world full of distractions, academic pressure, and constant digital noise, teenagers often struggle to manage their time, focus their attention, and juggle competing demands. Executive Functioning for Teens Made Simple by Juanita Finger arrives as a practical, encouraging, and teen-friendly guide to help them do precisely that—simplify, organize, and succeed.

Written in accessible language tailored specifically for teens, this book takes a direct, relatable approach to teaching executive functioning skills—those essential brain-based processes that help individuals plan, focus, remember instructions, and manage multiple tasks successfully. Finger doesn't bog readers down with clinical jargon. Instead, she offers straightforward advice and actionable steps that meet teens where they are, providing guidance that is both practical and relatable.

At its core, the book aims to "unclutter" both the physical and mental chaos that often clouds a teen's ability to focus on what matters—whether that's schoolwork, hobbies, friendships, or personal goals. With gentle humor and down-to-earth language, Finger helps teens understand the importance of routines, time-blocking, prioritization, and self-regulation. She also gives guidance on how to build supportive habits without turning life into a rigid schedule.

One standout feature of this guide is its emphasis on digital tools. Rather than asking teens to unplug entirely, Finger acknowledges their reality and suggests useful apps and strategies to leverage technology for productivity instead of distraction. From calendar management to focus-boosting techniques, the book embraces modern solutions while maintaining a grounded, human tone.

The final sections are especially valuable for those approaching graduation or preparing for college. Finger discusses how executive functioning challenges evolve with independence and provides tools to navigate this new territory with confidence. The advice is both practical and empowering—ideal for teens feeling overwhelmed by the transition.

Educators, parents, and counselors will also find this book to be a helpful resource, but its true strength lies in its voice: supportive without being preachy, informative without being condescending. It feels like advice from a wise, caring adult who understands teen life firsthand.

SAFE HAVEN
Peter Hargraves

Reviewer: Jeyran Main

Peter Hargraves' Safe Haven is a gripping, genre-blending science fiction adventure set in a hauntingly plausible post-apocalyptic future. With shades of espionage, survival, and resistance woven into a richly imagined world, the novel delivers a tightly paced and emotionally charged tale of escape and resilience.

Set in the 23rd century, after a fertility-crushing virus has decimated the global population and regressed society's technology to 1930s standards, Safe Haven follows Margaret, a woman trapped in a toxic and dangerous marriage. Her husband, Barran—deeply embedded in criminal networks—uses threats, surveillance, and control to ensure she doesn't leave. When she meets Jonathon, a mysterious but compassionate stranger, Margaret seizes the chance to break free, igniting a high-stakes chase that spans continents.

Hargraves skillfully balances this main plotline with a parallel story from a decade earlier. Wolfe, drafted by mistake into a brutal felon-only military unit, eventually escapes to Catamount—a sovereign country inhabited by genetically engineered, intelligent cougars. As Wolfe becomes part of the Catamount spy network, readers are presented with an alternate civilization emerging from humanity's collapse, one that reflects our own failings and future possibilities.

When these two threads finally converge—Margaret's growing suspicions and Jonathon's shocking revelation that he is Wolfe—the novel takes a sharp and thrilling turn. With the enemy closing in, the couple flees across dangerous terrain in a desperate bid for safety. From steam car escapes to fake passports and embassy hideouts, Hargraves keeps the tension taut, never sacrificing character for pace.

One of the novel's strengths lies in its worldbuilding. The juxtaposition of retro-futurism with genetic engineering feels both imaginative and grounded. The concept of intelligent, organized cougars leading a technological revival is bold, yet Hargraves handles it with sincerity and detail that makes it believable. The Catamounts aren't gimmicks—they're fully realized characters and cultural agents of change.

Margaret's evolution from passive victim to resourceful survivor adds emotional weight, and Wolfe is equally compelling as a man shaped by trauma, guilt, and ultimately, redemption.

PARTNER
David M. McGowan

Reviewer: Jeyran Main

Partners by David M. McGowan is a rugged, character-driven Western that delves deep into the human need for connection, even in the face of grief, distrust, and survival. With evocative prose and a stark portrayal of frontier life, McGowan crafts a poignant and emotionally layered story of unlikely companionship forged in the untamed wilds of the American West.

The novel centers on Thomas Brash, a man haunted by the memory of his family's death from cholera. Carrying the weight of that loss, Brash embarks on a solitary journey through a dangerous, lawless landscape—perhaps hoping the wild will erase the sorrow he cannot shake. Hardened by grief and determined to outrun his past, he lives by instinct, avoiding entanglements. But fate, as it often does, has other plans.

When he crosses paths with Frank Clement, a rough-edged, impulsive youth who seems his opposite in every way, Brash's carefully guarded solitude is unexpectedly disrupted. Their meeting sets in motion a slow, reluctant partnership born out of necessity but deepened by experience. What begins as a tense alliance evolves into something far more meaningful as they face hardship and danger together.

Brash views Clement as reckless and in need of guidance, while Clement sees Brash as strangely passive and overly cautious. The friction between them drives much of the story's emotional tension, but McGowan wisely balances this with moments of humor, tenderness, and mutual vulnerability. Their dynamic offers a compelling portrait of two wounded men growing not only as individuals but also as a pair learning to trust despite their fears.

As the story unfolds, the two encounter other wanderers and slowly form a makeshift community of loners, each carrying the scars of their past. For a time, it seems they may have found a kind of peace, but the ghosts of what they've endured inevitably return, testing their resolve and the strength of their fragile bonds.

McGowan's writing is vivid, immersive, and thoughtful. The landscape is more than a setting—it becomes a mirror of the characters' internal struggles: harsh, beautiful, and unrelenting. He embraces the spirit of the West while pushing beyond its familiar tropes, offering depth and a contemplative take on survival and redemption.

Partners reads like a modern classic—perfect for readers who appreciate literary Westerns with grit, heart, and introspection. It's a quiet yet emotionally powerful tale of resilience, loss, and the unexpected healing that can come through human connection.